SIFTED WORDS

TSADHE

(Truth Spoken Aligns Destiny He Elicited)

by

DR. RENEE' A. MEEKS

ISBN: 979-8-9875656-8-1

DEDICATION AND HONOR

The Bible declares "Honor your father and mother, Then you will live a long, full life in the land the Lord your God is giving you." Exodus 20:12(KJV)

Fannie Elnora Whisenant Jones, MY MOMMA or as I affectionately called her, in a LOUD VOICE, "MA"; by the way, she hated it; she was bougie and wanted me to call her MOTHER, lol. Raymond Atkins Jones, MY DADDY, was the coolest, classiest, best-dressing, handsomest man I know.

My momma was an educator, thus, my grades better be "A's and B's because, "when yo butt hits the seat everyday; they GIVE you a 'C' just because yo butt was in the seat". My Mom was ALWAYS a visionary, she taught me to have a vision; just create a plan, set your goal and put it to action.

My DADDY was a Maitre'd; working in Fine-dining establishments that "his Family" couldn't visit. My Dad taught me you can be "YOU" and still present yourself with class, dignity and honor no matter whose presence you find yourself among.

My parents lived out "LOVE through the good, bad, ugly and indifferent, with LOVE as the foundation. Who I am is because of the foundation they laid in my life. I MISS YOU EVERYDAY; you were the BEST PARENTS IN THE WHOLE WIDE WORLD. I know that God NEVER errors when He calls us to Himself. However, I Honor ALL the deposits of love, wisdom, knowledge, nurturing and empowering me to have and implement Vision. Thank you for teaching me about Jesus and His Love.

Aunt Beecher Beatrice Whisenant , yes, an educator for 63 years Lol! She has been Auntie/Momma ALL my life. She is the Auntie who loved traveling and always by car; she kept all the nieces and nephews during holidays and summers. However, she always empowered us with life lessons, is ALWAYS the ROCK whenever we encounter difficult seasons in life, took us to explore adventures like amusement parks, etc. yet infused us daily to believe we could accomplish ANYTHING.

SHE BELIEVES IN FAMILY. She has been "Momma" since my momma went home to be with the Lord and has NEVER left my side through all the UPS AND DOWNS OF LIFE. AUNT BEECHER, as she is "affectionately" known to ALLLLLLL the students she taught for 63 years and everyone that crossed her path in life. Even though Aunt Beecher, is SMART and will love you for life. BUT Baby she will get you ALL the way together. lolI love you for you ALWAYS being a shoulder to cry or lean on, a wall of protection and a security blanket through every season of my life.

Apostle Dr. Will A. Meeks

"And out of your reverence for Christ be supportive of each other in love. For wives, this means being devoted to your husbands like you are tenderly devoted to our Lord" Ephesians 5:22 (TPT) I don't think I have enough time to share everything I can say about 'MY HUSBAND," Apostle Dr. Will A. Meeks. We met in the summer of 1987 and on September 3, 1988 we became husband and wife. I can remember the FIRST time my eyes connected with your eyes; in my spirit I saw over your head like a rainbow and heard a whisper, "that's your husband." I answered back in my mind, "Girl sit down, just because the man single." Lol However, as I always. tell people all the time, this is the shortest yet longest relationship I have experienced in terms of man/woman relationships.

I want to tell you today honey, I thank God He gave us each other. You have always been such a protective covering in my life. Your Faith in God, was beyond MY comprehension when we first married, however your life of Prayer, fasting and belief that GOD CAN DO EVERYTHING, has and continues to manifest in our lives daily far above what I could think or imagine.

I am honored to be Momma to our children and grandchildren!!! You even blessed me to be a Sister and Auntie; I have no siblings so I never thought I would be an Auntie. II am grateful for the genuine love you have for all of my Family, even though you try to steal my Goddaughter, spiritual daughter and ALLLL my spiritual children!!!

I am honored that you and I are in covenant together with each other and especially with God that we do life through the "pass through storms, walk through fires, and open red seas – TOGETHER".

I love you for life!!!!!

WE ARE TESTIMONIES OF HIS MIRACLES OF MERCY

Table of Contents

Sifted Words

Truth Spoken Aligns Destiny He Elicited
TSADE

"SIFTED WORDS" - Tsadhe – "Truth Spoken Aligns Destiny He Elicited" is a Trust Builder – inner healer – Destiny Facilitator Book. This Book takes faith-filled Words directly from the scripture and "SIFTS" each letter in the word into an acronym that will break up the fallow ground of the enemy infiltrations of doubt, fear and unbelief embedded in our soul and spirit. The Bible declares "Thou shalt also decree a thing, and it shall be established unto thee. And the light shall shine upon thy ways." Thus, each day we empower our inward man by decreeing whichever acronym applies to the circumstances you are facing in this season; the fallow ground of the enemy is broken up and you are empowered with faith and strength to withstand the thoughts of the enemy and the light of God's presence, power, principles will release praise from your lips. PRAISE STILLS THE AVENGER!!!

Additionally, each day has a challenge of self-introspection entitled "What's the TEA?" - Thought – Emotion – Action. This allows us to be aware of the infiltrations in our inward parts that are deceptive and stagnate our belief system from aligning with faith-filled Words that align and lead to Destiny ordained by God.

Tsadhe in Hebrew represents the number 90 and represents a humble and faithful servant bent in submission. The word Tsadhe means "Righteous one." "SIFTED WORDS" is comprised of 90 acronyms and 90-days of "What's the TEA?"

DAILY TSADHE CHALLENGE:

WHAT'S THE TEA?

Let's break down how our thoughts, emotions, and actions reflect our understanding of our **royal** identity in Christ.

1. **T - THOUGHTS:**

   Reflect on what thoughts arise when you consider your **royalty** in God's Kingdom. Do you fully believe in your royal authority and identity, or are there doubts? Write down any inner thoughts you may have that challenge this belief. Example:

   "Can I really live in the authority and dignity of being part of God's royal priesthood? How do I carry myself with this identity in everyday life?"

   _____

   _____

   _____

   _____

   _____

2. **E - EMOTIONS:**

   Now that you've reflected on your thoughts, what emotions do these thoughts trigger? Do you feel empowered, or do you feel inadequate or doubtful? Name those emotions.

   Example:

   Confidence, but also uncertainty about living up to this role.

   _____

   _____

_____

_____

_____

3. **A - ACTIONS:**

How do these thoughts and emotions affect your actions? Do you find yourself living in boldness and faith, or do your doubts lead to hesitation and fear?

Example:

I sometimes hesitate to step into leadership roles because I don't feel equipped to represent God's royal priesthood.

_____

_____

_____

_____

_____

TSADHE Exercise

T - Truth | S - Spoken | A - Aligns | D - Destiny | H - He | E - Elicited

After identifying your thoughts, emotions, and actions, it's time to realign your mind with **God's truth** through the "TSADHE" challenge. Speak the truth of scripture over your life, countering any negative inner voices or emotions with God's promises.

Step 1: Create a truth based on scripture that relates to your **royal** identity and any personal challenges you may be facing.

Example Truth:

"I am a chosen generation, a royal priesthood, and I walk in the authority and dignity of the King of Kings. I show forth the praises of Him who called me into His marvelous light (1 Peter 2:9). I am not defined by my doubts or fears but by God's declaration over my life."

_____

_____

_____

_____

Step 2: Speak this truth out loud seven times a day, allowing it to **align** your thoughts and emotions with your **destiny** in Christ. Declare it consistently for three days.

_____

_____

_____

_____

_____

DECLARE:

Truth Spoken Aligns Destiny He Elicited

Speak the truth of your royal identity daily, allowing God's Word to shape your thoughts, emotions, and actions.

ROYAL

1 Peter 2:9-10

"But ye are a chosen generation, a royal priesthood, a holy nation, a peculiar people; that ye should show forth the praises of Him who hath called you out of darkness into His marvelous light."

Daily Acronym

Reverent Obeisance Yields Amazing Love

In God's kingdom, being **royal** is not just about status; it's about the responsibility to reflect the dignity, authority, and love of the King. As believers, we belong to a **royal priesthood**, called out of darkness to live in His marvelous light. This identity gives us **kingly power** and purpose, empowering us to walk in the authority of His Word.

Obeisance, which originally meant a vow of obedience, now signifies our humble submission and respect to the King of Kings. Every day, we should bow in **reverence** before God, honoring His unfailing love, protection, and provision. Our royal position in Him requires that we live in such a way that His praises are shown forth through us.

God's declaration over us as a **royal priesthood** is fixed—it transcends generations and circumstances. Whether facing trials or triumphs, this identity reminds us that we've been **chosen** and called to live with the power and authority He has given. We are set apart to show the world His glory.

Declaration:

I have been adopted into God's Kingdom. I walk in the authority of His Word, expressing dignity, understanding, and confidently declaring His power in the earth.

I am a royal priesthood!

APPLE

"Keep my commands and you will live; guard my teachings as the apple of your eye."

Daily Acronym

Amazing Promises Protection Last Eternally

One of the innumerable things I love about God and His Word—He never gives an instruction without releasing a blessing. We are all aware of the Word of God wherein God declares we are "the apple of His eye."

Today's scripture reference for "apple" encourages us: Do what I say, keep my commands, keep my words, store them up in your heart. Guard them, and you will live them.

Here comes the blessing: "And you will live well."

Guard them as the "apple of your eye."

Remember: "Apple" is symbolic of the forbidden. Make God's Word the apple of your eye and not forbidden from His sight.

A commandment is "a divine rule to be observed"; teaching is defined as "ideas or principles taught by an authority." When we live out His commandment and teaching as the "apple of your eye," God says, he who touches you touches the "apple of His eye."

LEAP

Psalm 18:29

"For by you I can run against a troop, by my God I can leap over a wall."

Daily Acronym

Live Expecting Answered Prayers

When we are in a season where we feel surrounded by a wall of opposition and the emotions of hopelessness are trying our faith, it's either breakdown or breakthrough.

To the naked eye and in our own strength, some of us, even though we are believers, will probably feel—and feeling, in and of itself, is not the instruction of God. Be encouraged to search the Word of God for a story where someone was boxed in with no possible way out. Fill your mind and soul with the Word of God to build your faith and always be reminded that God said, "With God, nothing is impossible." Ironically, God looks at those moments as an opportunity to show Himself strong and remind us, "Trust Me," not the voices or emotions which sound louder than My Word.

Remember: "I am the Lord of Hosts."

The word "hosts" is a translation of the Hebrew word "sabaoth," meaning "armies," referencing the angelic armies of heaven. Even when circumstances and situations in this life cause our emotions to exude the expression that we are facing a host or troop of enemies, always remember: By God's help, I am enabled to jump through, over, and land in a place of deliverance. LEAP!

FEAR

Isaiah 35:4

"Say to them that are of a fearful heart, Be strong, fear not: behold, your God will come with vengeance, even God with a recompense; He will come and save you."

Daily Acronym

Faith Empowers And Rewards

Fear is a word that defines our posture, and it has a two-fold meaning—the word is defined as awesome reverence and dreadful terror. It reminds us of the scripture in Deuteronomy 30:19, which begins, "Today I am giving you a choice of two ways..." As you experience difficulties and challenges in this life beyond your ability, choose to look in awesome reverence, knowing your God will come, and when He sees your choice, He will give you your reward.

Fear propels worry, doubt, and unbelief—in other words, we allow the enemy to steal, kill, and destroy the signs, miracles, and wonders of God, which are meant to be manifested through our test.

The Bible declares that God is a "very present" help in the time of trouble. Thus, when we understand, "Yes, I am in a season of testing that I do not have the ability to resolve on my own," we can say, "God, You said that when I run into Your presence, I will find a 'safe tower' and 'Faith Empowers And Rewards'."

During those seasons, the more we fill our thoughts, eye gate, and ear gate with the Word of God by reading and declaring, His presence will come with vengeance and flood our fearful heart with recompense and faith.

Choose to look in awesome reverence and dreadful terror, knowing your God will come and reward.

LOVE

Malachi 1:2 (ERV)

"The Lord said, 'I love you people.' But you said, 'What shows you love us?' The Lord said, 'Esau was Jacob's brother, but I chose Jacob.'"

Daily Acronym

Live Overcoming Valiantly Every day

This passage of scripture is synonymous with everyday life in the flesh—God has and continues to show His love for His creation. However, we don't even recognize it. Let's do an observation of our everyday lives when it comes to love. We view the dynamics of love according to how we see love through our own lens—our life experiences, i.e., hurts, disappointments, pain, joy. Thus, many times when people we say we love don't respond through our lens, we respond the same as today's scripture: "What shows you love us?" Oftentimes, there is no consideration for how their life experiences shape how they respond. "My way is right—that's it, that's all," and therefore, many relationships end in conflict and confusion without "in all your ways, get an understanding."

Jesus overcame to reassure us that we can overcome. Daniel, David, Gideon, Job, Rahab, the Prodigal Son—all overcame obstacles in life, and so can we.

The greatest display of love was when Jesus gave His life for us and told us, "Take heart, I have overcome the world... For every child of God defeats the world." Today and every day, be valiant and remind yourself that you can live overcoming valiantly every day and extend mercy to those you love, empowering them to love through His view.

SALT

Matthew 5:13

"You are the salt of the earth. But if the salt loses its taste, it cannot be made salty again. Salt is useless if it loses its salty taste. It will be thrown out where people will just walk on it."

Daily Acronym

Saved And Living Transformed

The Bible references salt in several metaphorical contexts, signifying purification, loyalty, usefulness, value, and permanence. Other references to the use of salt include it being a preserver—our lives should preserve the standards of God's Word. Salt is also a disinfectant; when mixed with water, many have rubbed salt over a wound, and the wound heals.

Many of us can attest to using salt to flavor our food and to heal infections.

I challenge every reader: identify the wounds in your life that you have tried and tried to heal to no avail. Jesus is a healer—take a leap of faith and allow God's Word to heal the wounds in your life. Hallelujah!

Salt is also referred to as a "covenant of friendship." Flavor your lives with just the right amount and sprinkle salt into the lives of your friends and loved ones, and watch God clean and heal their lives as well.

Since the Word of God instructs us to be witnesses of Him in all the earth, our saved and living transformed life is to be of use to God. Today, let someone taste and see His flavor in your life as we stand in permanent covenant with God and "salt the earth."

JOY

1 Samuel 2:1

"Hannah said, 'My heart is happy in the Lord; I feel very strong in my God. I laugh at my enemies. I am very happy in my victory.'"

Daily Acronym

Jesus Oils You

Truth be told, most of us associate joy with a feeling based on or in response to our present circumstances. However, in Isaiah 55:8-9, God has decreed, "For my thoughts are not your thoughts, neither are your ways my ways, saith the Lord."

The scripture for today clearly attests to the fact that circumstances don't dictate our mindset or posture in God. This story shows how Hannah is now rejoicing in God because, despite being taunted on a daily basis, she never moved from the posture that would give her victory. Think of all the ways she could have responded to her circumstances. This should encourage us that in the midst of any storm, we should saturate our belief system and mindset in prayer, praise, and expectation, trusting our God. This posture will always allow our dependency to be on God and not on ourselves. For the scriptures state, "The joy of the Lord is strength." My God, my God, my God.

The original Greek word for "joy" does not indicate that happiness is a prerequisite for what the world deems happiness. In addition to what the Bible describes as a "fruit of the Spirit," joy is a saturation of our spirit that illuminates our mind as a result of our relationship with the Lord. It allows us to exist with an inner assurance that exudes appreciation and rejoicing, knowing that our God has released healing, restoration, deliverance, and victory in every area of our life. Today and every day, allow the oil of joy to saturate your life.

DISCERN

Philippians 1:9-11 (NIV)

"And this is my prayer: that your love may abound more and more in knowledge and depth of insight, so that you may be able to discern what is best and may be pure and blameless for the day of Christ, filled with the fruit of righteousness that comes through Jesus Christ—to the glory and praise of God."

Daily Acronym

Developing Inner Checks Exuding Resolved Newness

When I reminisce about childhood times, I remember saying, "I can't wait until I get grown"—probably those thoughts came after being disciplined by my parents for something I felt was best for me, without understanding I was being selfish and lacked knowledge or understanding of the purpose of discipline and how it would shape my life, with or without it. Later in life, after making a decision to give my life to Jesus, here comes this discipline thing again. I came to know and understand that His discipline was just like parenting, yet on a whole new level.

Jesus, in His loving way, told us He wants us to become trees of righteousness that produce His fruit. Thus, that requires a choice to rid the tree of non-producing leaves.

Life will always present the choice: fruit or flesh. Discern.

We are on an everyday journey to become a reflection of the image of God in which we have been created. As such, discern signifies "to separate, to distinguish, as to investigate, determine, and decide one's condition—whether the thoughts and intents of one's heart are actually being lived out loud in daily choices." God is so gracious; He allows us the privilege and ability to look within and rely on the Holy Spirit to empower us to live out the resolved decision to be new in our hearts and minds to live to please Him. Today, decree and declare: I am made in the image of God, and I have the ability to develop inner checks exuding resolved newness, so that our love may abound more and more, and we will be able to discern what is best.

MIND

1 Chronicles 28:9 (NIV)

"And you, my son Solomon, acknowledge the God of your father, and serve him with wholehearted devotion and with a willing mind, for the Lord searches every heart and understands every desire and every thought. If you seek him, he will be found by you; but if you forsake him, he will reject you forever."

Daily Acronym

Making Intentional New Declarations

Favor, help, direction, power—the God whom we have committed to serve is omnipotent, omnipresent, and omniscient; He is strategic and does everything because He loves us and with His purpose in mind.

This scripture is a conversation between a loving father, David, who has experienced the extremities of being in right standing with God and making fleshly decisions outside the will of God. Yet, in all of his choices, he remained forever committed to God, acknowledging his faults and prayerfully asking God to create in him a clean heart.

Today, read the scripture above and replace Solomon's name with yours.

New thoughts—new intentions—new heart—new mind—new blessings.

He urges us to serve Him with undivided allegiance. He is a searcher of hearts and a willing mind. Please know—God is taking note of our intentions because He is in covenant with us and has promised that when we seek Him in faith, through prayer, meditation, reading, and obedience to His Word with a willing mind—He will be found by you.

"Make" means decided; "intentional" means willful. New declaration: I have willfully decided to love the Lord with all my heart, and I decree and declare favor, direction, and power. I am making intentional new declarations.

SEE

Matthew 5:8 (TPT)

"What bliss you experience when your heart is pure! For then your eyes will open to see more and more of God."

Daily Acronym

Seek Expect Experience

I believe most of us at some point in our lives have experienced eye drops to remove an infection or simply as an eyewash. The purpose of the experience was to bring clarity to the eyesight. However, in our relationship with God, in order to see God, our "sight" is cleansed or "purified" through allowing the "drops" of God's Word to "cleanse and purify" our "hearts." It seems like a dichotomy—"Words wash and purify my heart so I can see"—but God has established that His ways are not our ways. Furthermore, His sight is not just through our eyes, but through the heart.

Think: How many times and how many things have we seen through our eyes that led to hurt, pain, and disappointment?

Today, God is saying to us: Experience my ways—through prayer, reading, meditation, and worship—I will open the eyes of your heart and allow you to see where and how we need to purify it in order to align with my promises for your life. Expect and experience my sovereignty.

When we choose to walk with God daily, He refines us by purifying our hearts so that we may know Him and the power of His might. This purifying sets our desires and affections to see an inward change in our thoughts, desires, actions, responses, and experiences in life because we have made a decision to know Him. When we live in that posture and expectation, His glory shall be revealed to us and reflected in our lives. Seek, expect, and experience.

LIE

Numbers 23:19 (ESV)

"God is not a man, that he should lie, or a son of man, that he should change his mind. Has he said, and will he not do it? Or has he spoken, and will he not fulfill it?"

Daily Acronym

Live In Expectation

The story that aligns with today's daily acronym is a definitive reason for God's people to remain steadfast and unmovable in Him. Here is a man so consumed with "cursing what God had blessed" to the point that he was willing to pay a prophet of God to deceive. When we are not sure of the sovereignty and character of our God, we allow space for the deception of the enemy to announce a "lie" into and over our lives.

Thankfully, the prophet in this story had an ear not only to hear God but also to silence the loud voices of the enemy through his friend and remain steadfast in obedience to the voice of God. Even though there may be times in our lives when the "right now" blessing looks more appealing than the "wait on God" blessing, and we give in to the deception of the enemy, I encourage you today to study the Word of God. God says, "My sheep know my voice, and a stranger's voice they will not follow." When we don't know His voice, we believe the "lie."

It is the job of the enemy to bombard our minds (thoughts, decisions, and intellect) with doubt and unbelief about our almighty and all-powerful God. It is our humble submission to wake up every day and bombard our minds with the Word of God. We must become committed to hearing, believing, receiving, and trusting God's voice, spoken to us through reading, decreeing, and declaring or even listening to the Bible. Decide and abide in His Word, put your faith in action, and never doubt that "God is not like man, that He should lie." When He speaks through His Word, will He not then act? The next time the enemy brings the thought of his "lie," decree and declare out loud, "I live in expectation that God is not like man, that He should lie."

SIN

Proverbs 28:13 (GNT)

*"You will never succeed in life if you try to hide your sins.
Confess them and give them up; then God will show mercy to
you."*

Daily Acronym

Spirit Intercede Now

One of the many things I love about God is that He said, "He
without sin, cast the first stone," which makes it clear—sin is an equal
opportunity for all mankind. Additionally, He has declared there is no
temptation that is not common to man that He has not made a way of
escape.

Let's explore the scripture today:

1. He pronounces that success will never be ours if we try to hide
   our sins—notice He makes it clear we will experience sin.
2. Then He gives an instruction—confess them.
3. Give them up.

When we create a relationship with God through His Word,
the Holy Spirit will unction us as to times when we are tempted to stray
away from God and into sin. My admonishment would be: whenever
we sense the unction of the Holy Spirit, let that become our caution
light to say, "Spirit intercede now." Make this part of your everyday
life—whatever area and whenever He reveals to us areas to give up, He

strengthens us and extends overcoming mercy so that we can live successful lives filled with greatness.

The biblical word for sin denotes "the act or state of missing the mark." We should feel honored and loved knowing we serve a God so loving and merciful that He allows us the privilege to confess our sins and receive His forgiveness. What an awesome God! The scripture for today states, "You will never succeed in life if you try to hide your sins. Confess them and give them up; then God will show mercy to you." The Holy Spirit dwells within us! When we ignite that power to intercede on our behalf for strength, we receive just what we ask. Access the power within and decree and declare, "Spirit intercede now."

STRESS

Philippians 4:6 (NLT)

*"Don't worry about anything; instead, pray about everything.
Tell God what you need, and thank him for all he has done."*

Daily Acronym

Speak The Real Eternal Sovereign Scripture

Stress is defined as pressure, a state of mental or emotional strain or tension resulting from adverse or very demanding circumstances. Worry. The Bible clearly admonishes us that "the tongue has power"—speak to the mountain.

As people of God, yes, we have given our hearts to God in a covenant relationship, the power of His Word, yet many of God's people have not come to know, understand, believe, or test it in our everyday life experiences.

Let's be honest—the everyday challenges of life can be filled with stress—then we see in the scripture above—God's word tells us, "Don't worry about anything." Most of us would probably respond with two words, "For real, God?"—"How?"—like "You kidding, right?"—because we do not know, understand, or believe the power of His might.

In the same book, Philippians chapter 3, Paul said, "I want to know Christ and experience his mighty power." We know Him through His Word.

Today, I challenge you to follow the instructions in the scripture above. What words are your mouth filled with? Today's passage expresses: "Don't worry about anything; instead, pray about everything. Tell God what you need, and thank Him for all He has done." Choose to replace your worry with His Word. His words are spirit and life. Speak The Real Eternal Sovereign Scripture.

HUMBLE

1 Peter 5:6

"So humble yourselves under the mighty power of God, and at the right time he will lift you up in honor."

Daily Acronym

Hidden **U**nder **M**essiah's **B**ountiful **L**ove **E**veryday

The characteristics of "humble" in the Bible are: 1) prioritizing prayer; 2) wanting God's will, not yours; 3) putting others before yourself; 4) trusting Jesus; 5) obeying Him; 6) and knowing your limitations.

Recognize that God's power is mighty—as His children, we should be open to learning and adapting our lives to a posture that will position us for all the blessings He has already made available to us in His Word—be aware of our own strengths, weaknesses, shortcomings, and limitations. Choose to realign, renew, and reposition our will and mindset.

Sometimes we look at "humble" as a sign of weakness—however, God said, "In my weakness, He is my strength!"

Stay humble, and He will eventually exalt you—timing is in His hands!

The Bible says, "It's no longer I, but Christ (Messiah) that lives in me." When I understand that Christ the Messiah is love, and His love is generous, ample, abundant, free, magnanimous, and unselfish, I can, without reservation, be hidden or submitted to Him every day, knowing I am hidden under His mighty power, giving Him all my worries and cares, for He cares for me and He will lift me up in honor.

I choose to be hidden under Messiah's bountiful love every day!

SEED

Psalm 126:5-6

"Those who sow their tears as seeds will reap a harvest with joyful shouts of glee. They may weep as they go out carrying their seed to sow, but they will return with joyful laughter and shouting with gladness as they bring back armloads of blessing and a harvest overflowing."

Daily Acronym

Sow Expecting Extraordinary Deliverance

A seed is defined as the unit of reproduction.

Let's look at this in the spiritual realm—the scripture above states "those who sow their tears as seed will reap a harvest."

Now let's explore the natural—when a seed is planted in the ground, the soil has to be tilled before the seed is planted in order to have the capacity for producing the harvest. After the soil has been tilled and the seed is planted, it's now time to wait through the process—the process of watering, fertilizing, pulling weeds. You may not be able to see what the seed is doing—just know it is producing!

Today, clothe yourself with the seed of the Word of God. In tears, allow God to till your heart as the tears of seed drop into the ground of your pain—then, wait and process.

For the scripture today declares, "But they will return with joyful laughter and shouting with gladness as they bring back armloads of blessings and a harvest overflowing."

For it shall surely come to pass—sow expecting extraordinary deliverance.

WAITING

Psalm 27:14 (ESV)

"Wait for the LORD; be strong, and let your heart take courage; wait for the Lord!"

Daily Acronym

Worship And Intercede Trusting In Never-failing God

Waiting is defined as the action of staying where one is, watching, remaining, expecting, foreseeing, anticipating, tarrying, or abiding.

If truth be told, we don't like to wait for the red light to turn green. Waiting stirs up emotions such as anxiousness, frustration, anger, impatience, moodiness, just to name a few. Most times, the root of all these emotions is that we are not secure in what the outcome will be.

In today's scripture, notice we are not waiting on our friends or acquaintances—the instruction clearly states, "Wait on the Lord."

To "be strong" means:

1. Stand firm in knowing God will always come through.
2. Guard your heart—from the enemy's wiles trying to stir your emotions into discouragement and doubt.
3. Take action.

Worship and intercede in a never-failing God!

WEAPONS

2 Corinthians 10:4-5

"For although we live in the natural realm, we don't wage a military campaign employing human weapons, using manipulation to achieve our aims. Instead, our spiritual weapons are energized with divine power to effectively dismantle the defenses behind which people hide. We can demolish every deceptive fantasy that opposes God and break through every arrogant attitude that is raised up in defiance of the true knowledge of God. We capture, like prisoners of war, every thought and insist that it bow in obedience to the Anointed One."

Daily Acronym

Warfare Eases Annoying Pressures Ousting Nullifying Satan

"Strongholds," or as referred to in the scripture above, "arrogant attitudes," are directly tied to our thoughts, opinions, and allegiances. As believers, we must "stand firm" in knowing, believing, and declaring with expectation the power of God's Word to tear down "any" opposition to His Word, especially concerning His children.

Furthermore, we have a role in the fight:

1. Assess our thoughts to determine if they align with or oppose the Word of God.
2. Once we determine what is going on in our thoughts, posture ourselves for "war."

3. Begin to declare and meditate on scriptures that align against the "arrogant attitude."

4. Expect the power of God's Word to bring victory.

Weapons are defined as a means of gaining an advantage or defending oneself in a conflict or contest. As believers, the weapons of our warfare are the Word of God and prayer, along with the influence of God's omnipotence. God has instructed us that these weapons are mighty and pull down and demolish strongholds of doubt, unbelief, and all sorts of voices influenced by Satan. Ask yourself a question: What can defeat the Word of God? What has more power than God and His Word? He promised His Word would never return void. Today, use your weapons—go into warfare, ease annoying pressures, oust, and nullify Satan.

HOPE

Micah 7:7 (NIV)

"But as for me, I watch in hope for the Lord, I wait for God my Savior; my God will hear me."

Daily Acronym

His Omnipotence Provides Everyday

I love the fact that God always allows us a choice. He clearly establishes His position of power and sovereignty. He states, "I set before you life and death, choose."

Today's scripture is a reminder of being in a position where you don't have the power to change your circumstances, yet you are undecided as to whether or not to believe God can and will change you.

I humbly submit to you—watch in hope for the Lord. He doesn't lie, He can't fail, and if His Word said it—He can do it!

We live in a society where the world around us is filled with weariness, sadness, frustration, and corruption, to say the least. However, the Bible informs us, "Be not conformed to this world." Thus, we have a choice, and that choice requires us to decide, "I will look unto the Lord." Yes, decree it again, "I WILL look unto the Lord." Put no trust in man—the Bible declares a man's enemies are the men of his own house. When we look to the Lord, it floods us with a mindset of hope—God hears us. Choose to set our posture to look unto the Lord and wait for the God of our salvation. Remember and decree—His omnipotence provides every day.

PRAISE

Psalm 8:2 (ERV)

"From the mouths of children and babies come songs of praise to you. They sing of your power to silence your enemies who were seeking revenge."

Daily Acronym

Praise Releases Anointing Interrupts Satan's Efforts

Many times, as "kingdom citizens," we underrate the power of "praise." Praise is a posture, a position or stance where we KNOW AND UNDERSTAND that our Father is not limited to Savior—He is also protector, provider, defender, and keeper, among so many other things.

When we halle His name, we honor Him not only for His love, mercy, and grace, which He gives us new every morning, but we also give Him glory as we remember His benefits of healing, forgiveness, and present help—even in spite of trials, tests, trouble, and temptations.

It reminds me of the old saying, "When praises go up, blessings come down." As we take a posture to praise our God, the blessings of strength to know that our God never fails empower us to withstand the wiles of the enemy. David was between the age of 13–15 when he slew the giant Goliath! What is hindering your praise?

Our God is so powerful, yet loving, that He created the opportunity and privilege to exalt His name and to express gratitude for His worth. Even when children and babies praise Him with the fruit of their lips—not only does He hear, but He also stills the enemy and brings an end to the enemy's purposes. Praise has benefits—Praise Releases Anointing Interrupts Satan's Efforts. Don't start your day without it!

NEW

Lamentations 3:22-24

*"It is of the Lord's mercies that we are not consumed, because
his compassions fail not. They are new every morning: Great is
thy faithfulness. The Lord is my portion, saith my soul;
therefore, will I hope in him."*

Daily Acronym

Never Ending Worship

"New," translated in the Old Testament, is "Chadhash"—
meaning "bright," "fresh," "new."

The scripture above informs us that "every day" we wake up to
another day—Elohim Chaseddi, "the God of mercy,"—who withholds
harsh treatment that He has the right to inflict, allowing the
opportunity to obtain forgiveness through repentance.

That alone should ignite "Never Ending Worship," because we
recognize the gravity of the Lord's compassions toward us.

Today's Bible verse begins with the word "because"—
everything else occurs "because" of the Lord's great love. Thus, my
challenge to you is to extend the same to others.

Remember: The Lord chooses to show us His faithful love every
day "because." And thus, our choice should be a life of Never Ending
Worship—why? "Because."

PRIDE

Daniel 5:20

"But when his heart was lifted up, and his mind hardened in pride, he was deposed from his kingly throne, and they took his glory from him."

Daily Acronym

Puffed Righteousness Inhibits Deliverance Exacerbates

There are so many scriptures that remind us, "I give you power to get [wealth, strength, wisdom]…" yet many times in our "flesh," we desire to be seen as "accomplished"—forgetting that "it is not we of ourselves, but Christ who lives in us." There is good news—this is not new to God!

I am reminded of King Saul in the Old Testament, who was driven to downfall because of his pride. King Nebuchadnezzar, though he was smart, was very proud and thought highly of his self-importance. Ananias died on the spot and was carried out because of his pride. Suffice it to say, the scripture is correct—pride comes before a fall.

Life lessons have taught me to continue growing in following the Bible's instructions to "search and try our ways." Ask questions like: Have I lost sight of the fact that it is God propelling me to obtain His overabundance of blessings, or do I believe I obtained it on my own? Awareness is the first step in turning back to the right posture. Have I become so consumed that I no longer pray, read my Bible, or spend time in God's presence because I now depend on me?

Throughout the Bible, we are constantly reminded of how Jesus remained lowly and humble in spirit, especially knowing He is the Son of Almighty God! Jesus led by example! The Bible instructed and admonished the men and women who served and were used by God to follow Jesus' example. As people of God, even in our excitement and awe of knowing that God is using us, it is imperative that we constantly do a heart and mind check-up. Puffed Righteousness Inhibits Deliverance Exacerbates.

DOUBT

Jude 1:22 (ESV)

"And have mercy on those who doubt."

Daily Acronym

Dismiss Oppression Undergirding Biblical Truths

Doubt is defined in the Bible as wavering between two minds or lacking confidence, assurance, or complete trust in God. It is a deviation from the truth about God in thought or deed.

The discipline of learning that we do NOT have to "doubt" God is an ongoing journey in our walk with Him. The Bible tells us that our flesh "wars" against our spirit. We know this well, as God gave an instruction to Adam and Eve about what to eat and what not to eat. Yet the voices of deception spoke so loudly in Eve's mind that she submitted her will to the voice in her head and not the clear instruction from God.

A daily practice in our lives should be to declare the decree, "My sheep know my voice, and a stranger's they will not follow."

Along this journey, I have come to understand—when I am in a season of testing or trial or temptation and my spirit reveals to me, "You are in a place of doubt," I take heed because in that moment, I realize I have backed away from the presence of God where mercy and grace build my capacity to receive, and now I'm walking through this journey in my own strength. Doubt receives nothing.

When you find yourself in that place, as we all do, cry out, "I believe—help my unbelief!" Respond—Dismiss Oppression Undergirding Biblical Truths!

PRAY

Philippians 4:7 (NLT)

"Don't worry about anything; instead, pray about everything. Tell God what you need, and thank Him for all He has done. Then you will come to experience God's peace, which exceeds anything we can understand. His peace will guard your hearts and minds as you live in Christ Jesus."

Daily Acronym

Praying Returns Abundant Yields

Today's scripture "clearly" states: "Pray about everything."

When Jesus became flesh and walked among men, though He had been given "authority" by His Father, He would continually "pray" to His Father about "everything." Unfortunately, in our human nature, we often appear "self-sufficient," which creates an inward conflict in trusting and relinquishing our independence to conform to the will of God. Jesus' example serves as a perfect model for us to hold fast to, as He shows that even in the flesh:

1. Dependence on God is crucial
2. Trust in God's ability to hear and answer is necessary
3. Jesus left an example for us to follow, and He has no respect of persons.

"Pray" is defined as a solemn request or plea, to plead, invoke, ask, or supplicate.

PRAY ABOUT EVERYTHING—good, bad, ugly, indifferent, friends, and enemies! If we ask anything according to His will, He hears us. And if we know that He hears us, whatever we ask, we know that we have the petitions that we desired of Him. Don't start or end your day without it—Praying Returns Abundant Yields!

REAP

Galatians 6:9 (TPT)

"And don't allow yourselves to be weary in planting good seeds, for the season of reaping the wonderful harvest you've planted is coming!"

Daily Acronym

Receiving Enlargement And Prosperity

This scripture reminds me of the farmer—he "prepares the soil" and "plants the seed in the ground." When I think about the fact that the farmer plants with the mindset of putting the seed in the ground "knowing" the seed "will" reap a harvest.

I encourage you today—stop wondering "if, when, how."

In the verse right above today's scripture, the Word states, "The harvest you reap reveals the seed that YOU planted…"

QUESTION: What does my harvest reveal about the seeds I have planted?

Take time to re-adjust your mindset and expectation—"Don't allow yourselves to be weary…" Even mustard seed faith will allow you to reap a bountiful harvest.

"Reap" means to receive (a reward or benefit) as a consequence of one's own or other people's actions. Most of us have heard the saying, "The end of a thing is better than the beginning!" A great example, especially for today's word, would be the life of a farmer—he sows the seed, then he has to take care of the ground in which the seed was sown because he sowed with the expectation of reaping a reward. When harvest time arrives, what the farmer will reap is far more than he sowed. When we live for the Lord, our everyday life is a seed lived out in His presence. Ask yourself—what will my life reap in this season? Live each day pleasing God, then you can expect to be Receiving Enlargement And Prosperity!

INCREASE

Psalm 115:14

"The Lord shall increase you more and more, you and your children."

Daily Acronym

Indelible Non-Decreasing Concepts Revealed Escalating Augmented Strong Enlargement

Increase denotes growth, enlargement, expansion, and elevation.

One of the many ways God gives "increase" is by increasing the power of the Holy Spirit in our lives to withstand the ploys of the enemy to steal, kill, and destroy every area of our lives. He increases the Spirit of God in us to prompt faith, hope, love, joy, patience, gentleness, and humility. And He said He won't stop at "increase" in your life—He will "increase" your children. Can we say—Generational Blessings!

RIGHT NOW—I feel a "That I may know Him and the power of His might" praise—Enlarge My Territory!

Notwithstanding, He will increase our wealth, riches, and honor!

When we make a choice to include the "Bread of Life" as part of our "Daily Bread," the Word becomes an "indelible" part of our mindset and we increase in every area of our lives—faith, fruit, and fulfillment. "Give us each day our daily bread"—Have you had your "Daily Bread" today?

Never forget the Word—Indelible Non-Decreasing Concepts Revealed Escalating Augmented Strong Enlargement—Shout INCREASE!

STORMS

Isaiah 25:4

"But you are a tower of refuge to the poor, O Lord, a tower of refuge to the needy in distress. You are a refuge from the storm and a shelter from the heat. For the oppressive acts of ruthless people are like a storm beating against a wall."

Daily Acronym

Stand Trusting Obedient Relentless Manifestation Sure

Just saying the word "storms" often comes with the forethought of disaster! However, let's delve into what God's definition of "storms" represents in our lives spiritually.

The Biblical meaning of "storms" can represent many different things. Non-destructive wind is an apt picture of the presence of God because God is powerful, yet unseen; scripture described the presence of God in the form of the "Holy Spirit" as the sound of a "mighty rushing wind."

In the natural, that same "mighty rushing wind" can sometimes end in disaster, but spiritually, it empowers people.

Today's scripture is a reminder that our God is mighty to save. In the midst of "storms," He allows us to do a checklist of our mindset—trust vs. doubt; prayer life—dull or thriving. And He reminds us that though the storm is raging, stay in the boat—you will make it to the other side! I AM ON THE BOAT!

Let's declare together: Safe, Shelter, Shade, Refuge. Whenever we are in the season of storms, we have the assurance along with evidence that "even the wind and the waves obey HIS VOICE." No matter the attack by a cruel enemy, God's power is fierce and sovereign! He WILL silence the enemy. Stand Trusting Obedient Relentless Manifestation Sure!!

DESTINY

Isaiah 46:10

*"Only I can tell you the future before it even happens.
Everything I plan will come to pass, for I do whatever I wish."*

Daily Acronym

Declaring Everyday Sacred Truths Impacting New Yearnings

Today's scripture is a reminder of the sovereignty of our God. Now my question is, why, when we hear a statement like this, do most mindsets go straight to negative thoughts? **Say amen!** Remember, in Jeremiah, God reminds us again: "For I know the plan, and my plan is not to harm you…"

He gave us the Holy Bible and made it known to us—when we declare a thing (His written Word), it **shall** be established. His Word is a roadmap to our destiny, in spite of the pitfalls, obstacles, ups, downs, good, bad, ugly, and indifferent. Anytime His Word is declared diligently and continually in faith, He establishes and brings His Word to pass. **Destiny.**

Have you yet to understand the power of His Word as it relates to the destiny He has birthed in you? He is waiting for the light of confidence, honor, and trust in us to "flip the switch" and turn on **every promise of God.**

Surrender is the heartbeat of destiny. When we submit our will to the will of God—strategically and intentionally developing into His image, allowing the Word of God to be our roadmap along this journey—our life becomes an outward expression and witness of His love and sovereignty. He, in turn, not only becomes our provision, but in return for our submission, the inner yearnings of our wants and desires begin to manifest. Remember, He declared the end from the beginning, and His plan **will** be realized. Don't stop—stay on course—Declaring Everyday Sacred Truths Impacting New Yearnings.

AWAKE

Isaiah 52:1

"Awake, awake, Zion, clothe yourself with strength! Put on your garments of splendor, Jerusalem, the holy city. The uncircumcised and defiled will not enter you again."

Daily Acronym

Alert Worshiping And Kneeling Everyday

Even though we are believers in Jesus Christ, there are moments and times in our journey when God needs to remind us to **awake.** The word "awake" suggests that we are asleep. "Awake" means to bestir, revive, or rouse from a state of inaction; to be invigorated with new life, as the mind awakes from its stupor.

Clearly, the inference is not related to sleeping in the natural. When our mindset is cluttered with the cares of this life, our emotional state exudes an aura of hopelessness, doubt, worry, and anxiousness. Here, God is reminding us—"wake that mind up from the stupidity." The stupidity of **unbelief.**

Today and every day—"Clothe yourself with strength!" The "strength" of the "garments" He has given His beloved. Clothe yourself with prayer and reading His Word, and shift your mindset from your circumstance to the power of an Almighty God who will **never** allow His people to be defeated!

The Lord is so gracious in His love toward us. In Isaiah 52:1, He reaffirms that when we "clothe ourselves with strength," even in the midst of situations and circumstances that appear too hard for us to bear, we will have inner peace and resilience to **be still and know He is God.**

Clothe yourself with Alert Worshiping And Kneeling Everyday!

SEX

1 Corinthians 6:16-20 (MSG)

There's more to sex than mere skin on skin. Sex is as much spiritual mystery as physical fact. As written in Scripture, "The two become one." Since we want to become spiritually one with the Master, we must not pursue the kind of sex that avoids commitment and intimacy, leaving us more lonely than ever—the kind of sex that can never "become one." There is a sense in which sexual sins are different from all others. In sexual sin we violate the sacredness of our own bodies, these bodies that were made for God-given and God-modeled love, for "becoming one" with another. Or didn't you realize that your body is a sacred place, the place of the Holy Spirit? Don't you see that you can't live however you please, squandering what God paid such a high price for? The physical part of you is not some piece of property belonging to the spiritual part of you. God owns the whole works. So let people see God in and through your body.

Daily Acronym

Sacred Entanglements Exclusively

The world has emphatically reduced sex to a sensual encounter (a casual meeting) of flesh.

Let's look to the Bible—"There's more to sex than mere skin on skin. Sex is as much a spiritual mystery as a physical fact. As written in Scripture, 'The two become one.' Since we want to become spiritually one with the Master, we must not pursue the kind of sex that avoids commitment and intimacy, leaving us lonelier than ever—the kind of sex that can never 'become one.' There is a sense in which sexual sins are different from all others. In sexual sin, we violate the sacredness of our own bodies—these bodies that were made for God-modeled love, for 'becoming one' with another. Or didn't you realize that your body is a sacred place, the place of the Holy Spirit? Don't you see that you can't live however you please, squandering what God paid such a high price for? The physical part of you is not some piece of property belonging to the spiritual part of you. God owns the whole work. So let people see God in and through your body."

As seen clearly from the Bible, sex is a **sacred creation** of Almighty God.

The word **entangle** in the Bible is defined as to complicate, to enmesh, to twist or interweave in such a manner as not to be easily separated, to make tangled.

Be mindful—sex was created by God and is designed to provide pleasure and satisfaction. It has been given as a gift to be experienced for pleasure and delight within marriage, as it complements and enhances the relationship of love.

Be watchful of your **entanglements!**

BOLDLY

Hebrews 4:16

"So now we draw near freely and boldly to where grace is enthroned, to receive mercy's kiss and discover the grace we urgently need to strengthen us in our time of weakness."

Daily Acronym

Believing Our Lord Delivers, Let's Yield

This passage of scripture reminds me of a song we sang in church when I was a child—"What a friend we have in Jesus, all our sins and griefs to bear, what a privilege to carry everything to God in prayer." The scripture **never** mandated a certain state of mind or standing in Christ when we come to Him.

Jesus Christ, in His always loving manner towards His creation, extends an invitation: **Come, draw near, freely, boldly!** Just **knowing** this ought to cause us to lift our hands in honor and praise to our loving God! He did not leave **me** out when He extended the invitation.

Furthermore, since we **know** He extended the invitation, read further—He wants to **give** us mercy, to extend to us grace and strength in our weakness.

The Word of God clearly encourages us to come—and thus, do so boldly! There are moments in our journey when the weight of testing and trials overwhelms our minds, and we lose sight of the fact that God **never** intends to harm us or fail us! In those moments, come back into His presence, acknowledging, "I cannot fix this situation; I need You, Lord." In that moment, remember, "I'm still on the journey, and He has not failed me yet." Be bold enough to ask Him for what you need without fear so that we may receive mercy and grace in our time of need.

Come—Believing Our Lord Delivers, Let's Yield!

PAIN

1 Chronicles 4:9 (AMP)

"Jabez was more honorable than his brothers; but his mother named him Jabez, saying, 'Because I gave birth to him in pain.'"

Daily Acronym

Past Afflictions Incubating Newness

Pain—spiritually—is not just anger toward God because of a season of testing or trials. It can sometimes be the result of inner conflict about various life experiences (i.e., the lady with the issue of blood, Joseph's brothers selling him, or the two women who decided to eat each other's children to survive). Thus, we do not really know if Jabez's mother's pain was limited to childbirth.

Given the fact that a **name** is **your identity**, and the Word of God says, "we have what we say," this is a clear example of passing on a generational curse. Imagine, every time you hear your name being called, they are saying, "Hello, Pain."

This is a **good place** to thank and honor God, because **any** situation or circumstance He allows in our lives **always** has His purpose attached. We know God said His plan is **not** to harm us. He reveals that even in Jabez's life. The Bible says Jabez was an "honorable" man, so he understood how to **honor** God. He didn't allow the **name/identity** attached to his life to stifle his future. He honored and sought God for deliverance in his circumstances.

Today—identify what **past pains** have caused you to see yourself out of alignment with who **God** says you are. Then draw strength from the fact that when Jabez changed his thoughts about his identity and sought the Lord for what he wanted his life to speak, the Bible says, "And God did just what he asked."

Identify your past afflictions and allow God to incubate (develop) newness in your life. **God will do just what He said!**

TEST

Psalm 66:10

"For You, O God, have tested us; You have tried us as silver is tried."

Daily Acronym

Trials Empower Stabilize Transformation

Oftentimes, as believers, we think or assume that Satan, the enemy, or the deceiver has brought **all** of the tests in our lives. However, today's scripture reminds us, **"You, O God, have tested us."**

Even further, in Malachi 3:10 (AMP), God says, "Bring all the tithes (the tenth) into the storehouse, so that there may be food in My house, and test Me now in this, says the Lord of hosts... " **I love** that God says, "Test Me"—'I know who I am and what I can do.'

Let's not just focus on the emotional rollercoaster we sometimes **feel** like we're on because we're not standing in the **posture of God is able to do anything**—even if it looks impossible to the naked eye. Additionally—every day, throw your hands up in honor and praise, and declare, **"With God, all things are possible—Lord, this is not too hard for You."**

Trust God's sovereignty—know, understand, and believe that this is not too hard for You, O Lord. You are developing my innermost being to withstand the wiles of the enemy!

Declare—Trials Empower Stabilize Transformation!

TEMPTATION

1 Corinthians 10:13

"No temptation [regardless of its source] has overtaken or enticed you that is not common to human experience [nor is any temptation unusual or beyond human resistance]; but God is faithful [to His word—He is compassionate and trustworthy], and He will not let you be tempted beyond your ability [to resist], but along with the temptation He [has in the past and is now and] will [always] provide the way out as well, so that you will be able to endure it [without yielding and will overcome temptation with joy]."

Daily Acronym

Today Enforce Messiah's Promises Triumphantly, Annihilating Temptation's Infiltration, Omnipresence Nullifies

The lure of what is forbidden is common to **all** mankind:

- It is **not** beyond human resistance.
- It will **always** provide a way out.
- You will develop the fruit of endurance.
- God **will** provide a way out of temptation.
- You do not have to yield to the temptation.
- You **will** overcome with joy.

We are so blessed to know that God's method of teaching is completely different from mankind's. Whenever temptation appears challenging to your flesh, **declare**—"This is not beyond my ability to resist" and "God has given me a way out."

OVER

Psalm 106:43

*"Over and over God rescued them, but they never learned—
until finally, their sins destroyed them."*

Daily Acronym

Opposition Vigilantly Eradicated and Reversed

As believers with a heart and mind made up to serve the Lord, the reality is that we **will** face obstacles and opposition—**over and over** along this journey. Most of us would read this and think the obstacles and opposition are coming from "haters," which can be true to a degree.

Today's scripture, however, is referring to the ongoing struggle between our flesh and spirit, the **internal** war concerning the choices of the soul. Let's look further into today's scripture.

The verse reiterates that God rescued "them/us" over and over. Yet it goes on to say, **"But they never learned, until it destroyed them."**

This is how much we are loved—"Still, when God saw the trouble they were in and heard their cries for help, He remembered His covenant with them, and His immense love took them by the hand. He poured His mercy on them while their captors looked on, amazed."

Along this journey, we will face internal and external opposition.

Cry for help—He hears—Opposition Vigilantly Eradicated and Reversed!

ADVERSITY

Proverbs 24:10 (ESV)

"In the day of prosperity, be joyful, and in the day of adversity consider: God has made the one as well as the other, so that man may not find out anything that will be after him."

Daily Acronym

A Divine Victorious Enablement Restoring Situations Intended Toward You

Adversity is defined in the Bible as an event, or series of events, that oppose success or desire; misfortune, calamity, affliction, distress; a state of unhappiness.

The key words in today's scripture: "Consider: God made the one as well as the other."

Oftentimes, we assume that **all** adversity is coming directly from Satan. However, God **never** allows situations or circumstances in our lives that He is not sovereign to handle. Understand—**everything** He allows us to experience has His purpose attached to it, and it is always for our growth and development in the things of God.

Remember: His ways are **not** our ways, yet He never allows an experience in our journey to cause harm, per Jeremiah 29:11. Prosperity, as well as adversity, is **all** part of **His plan**.

Moses, Joseph, Ruth, David, Jeremiah, and others are examples to assure us that in and through adversity, **God never leaves us**—He develops His character in us through the situation, and we **will** come through the adversity victorious!

DILIGENT

Psalm 64:6

"They search out iniquities; they accomplish a diligent search; both inward thought of every one of them and the heart is deep."

Daily Acronym

Divinely Irrefutable Love Inducing God's Empowering Never-ending Trust

In our everyday lives, being diligent is key to being successful in all we put our hands to do. It is no different in the Kingdom of God. Since we are in a forever covenant relationship with God, to truly know in whom we believe, we must **learn** of Him, and as we learn of Him, He reveals both our inward and outward parts.

The Bible says it's not what goes into a man that defiles him, but what comes out. Jesus, our perfect example, frequently sought the Lord away from the crowd and distractions.

Jesus understood He could do **nothing** without God. Unfortunately, we live in a time where "self-love" and "my truth" dominate. However, God's Word decrees—He desires **truth** on the inward parts. That truth is His Word, and with the Holy Spirit's help, it will lead us and guide us into **all truth.**

Today—Search your inward parts—do they align with God's Word? Wherever they are not aligned, pull off the old man. We serve a loving God who is waiting to hear our cry. Diligence is a virtue that defines thoroughness, completeness, and persistence in action.

God rewards those that diligently seek Him.

REST

Psalm 62:1

"Truly my soul finds rest in God; my salvation comes from Him."

Daily Acronym

Renewed Elevated Stabilized Trust

Rest means peace, ease, or refreshment.

Rest is an **intentional** mindset and act of confidence in our Lord and Savior. In today's world, everything is about hurrying and rushing. As the older generation used to say, "You're going nowhere fast." However, as we journey through life with God, **He is time** and **all things happen in His time**.

When we make it a discipline to spend **daily** time in the presence of God, He calms the hurriedness and anxiousness of our hearts and minds. As we know, when we face dire circumstances and situations, our emotions are on high alert with "What if?"—What if God can't do what I'm asking? What if I'm not good enough? What if He doesn't come on time, and I lose everything? These thoughts can trigger doubt, unbelief, and discouragement.

Today, I encourage and remind you (and myself), God's Word is His covenant promise to His children. Make time in His presence a part of your day every day. Even when your mind and emotions are bombarded with thoughts that don't align with His Word, run to His presence—it's a safe tower. There, you will find that **He is working everything for your good.**

REST—Renewed Elevated Stabilized Trust!

FACT

James 1:19

"My dearest brothers and sisters, take this to heart: Be quick to listen, slow to speak, and slow to become angry, for human anger is never a legitimate tool to promote God's righteous purpose."

Daily Acronym

Fresh Anointed Christian Truths

Today is truly a day of transparency! When the Lord dropped the acronym for the word "FACT" into my spirit, I had **no idea** that the word "fact" does not appear in the Bible except as a heading in the KJV (2 Kings 10) and as a reference to the fact (deed) regarding the murder of Onias in 2 Maccabees 4:36. Thus, this was definitely a revelation from God.

However, the difference between **truth** and **fact** in the Bible is that "truth" is understood as a person—it is God Himself. **Facts**, on the other hand, have a firm basis in reality, and therefore are important.

So I kept searching and found five scriptures that mention "facts": Luke 1:3, Acts 24:13, Acts 18:25, Acts 21:34, and Acts 25:7 (in the Basic English Bible translation).

What did I learn? Be slow to anger—God's **truth** is always based on **facts** that will be revealed. They truly are:

Fresh Anointed Christian Truths!

IGNITE

Psalm 2:12 (HCSB)

"Pay homage to the Son or He will be angry, and you will perish in your rebellion, for His anger may ignite at any moment. All those who take refuge in Him are happy."

Daily Acronym

Initiate Godly Needed Infallible Truths Effectively

When I look at this scripture, several things stand out:

1. Honor God
2. God's anger
3. Be mindful of our rebellious ways
4. The speed and magnitude of God's anger
5. Those who trust God find refuge
6. He always blesses His children, even in times of chaos and anger

I encourage you to make sure to keep the **fire of God ignited** in your life through His presence, His Word, prayer, worship, and fellowship—**by all means necessary.** Staying ignited in your daily walk will keep you protected, alert to the ways of God, and away from a life of rebellious ways that are **not** of God.

In one passage of scripture, God said, "They will know that I am the Lord when I ignite a fire in Egypt, and all her allies are defeated."

Keep yourself from the wrath of an angry God!

Initiate Godly Needed Infallible Truths Effectively.

CUP

Psalm 23:5-6 (TPT)

"You become my delicious feast even when my enemies dare to fight. You anoint me with the fragrance of your Holy Spirit; you give me all I can drink of You until my cup overflows."

Daily Acronym

Christ's Undeniable Promises

Throughout Scripture, the **cup** operates as a metaphor for an individual's **fate**.

We can attest in Psalm 16:5—"Lord, You alone are my portion and my cup; You make my lot secure"—and in Matthew 23:25—"…You clean the outside of the cup and dish, but inside they are full of greed and self-indulgence."

Additionally, Scripture tells us in Psalm 116:13, "I will take the cup of salvation and call upon the name of the Lord"; and in 1 Corinthians 11:25, "This cup seals the new covenant with My blood. Drink it—and whenever you drink this, do it to remember Me."

Which **cup** are you drinking from so that your life might be filled to overflowing? As believers, we have been graciously given freedom of **choice**, even in the Kingdom. Understand, whatever cup we drink from and **fill** our lives with will reap a harvest.

I admonish you: "You give me **all** I can drink of You until my cup overflows."

All of God's promises are **Yes** and **Amen**. He watches over His Word to perform it. What area of your life do you need to fill with Christ's undeniable promises?

REBELLIOUS

Deuteronomy 31:27 (AMP)

"For I know your rebellion and contention and your stubbornness; behold, while I am still alive with you today, you have been rebellious against the Lord; how much more, then, after my death?"

Daily Acronym

Recalcitrant Enforcement Binds Entraps Long-suffering, Lord Invoke Our Undefeated Savior

Rebellion is more than being ignorant of God's ways or being independent—it is the act of **not obeying His commands** or being submissive to divinely appointed authorities, instead choosing to go one's own way.

As children of the Most High God, we must understand and accept that He **knows all** and **sees all**. Even when we try to present ourselves in ways that make it seem like we didn't know better or were unaware of His commandments concerning a matter, God **knows** whether or not we are being transparent and honest.

Even when we err, God is faithful and just to forgive us when we take ownership and acknowledge Him in all our ways. The Bible says, "Let us search and try our ways and turn again to the Lord."

Today—Search inwardly: Have I been recalcitrant, willingly walking in my own will, unaware that I am allowing the enemy to keep me bound from the blessings of God?

Trust—rebellious ways will never profit you anything.

PATIENCE

James 1:2 (NKJV)

"My brethren, count it all joy when you fall into various trials, knowing that the testing of your faith produces patience."

Daily Acronym

Promises Activated Through Intense Endurance Need Courage Elevated

Patience is the ability to endure difficult people and situations without giving in to anger or giving up hope. Yet, I'm always amazed at how much we want God to have **patience** with us, but we are often **impatient** with others.

Trust me, I know full well that patience is not only a fruit that takes time to ripen, but also a virtue, which nowadays seems rare. Many people claim to be accepting of "my truth," but the Bible clearly says we shall know the **truth**—God's **Word**—and His truth will set us free.

Today's scripture clearly states:

- Count it **joy** when you fall into **various** trials;
- **Knowing** that the testing of your faith **produces** patience;

The key factor is that God is not trying to harm or destroy us in this situation. Instead, He is producing in us the patience to **trust** that He will deliver us from the hand of the enemy. When we approach our situations in **faith** and **confidence**, we inquire of God what level of endurance He is producing in our lives through patience.

WEALTHY

Psalm 66:10-12

"For You, O God, have tested us; You have tried us as silver is tried. You brought us into the net; You laid affliction upon our loins. You have caused men to ride over our heads; We went through fire and through water; but You brought us out into a wealthy place."

Daily Acronym

Wisdom Empowered Aligning Life Through Him YES

If I were to take a vote and ask, "Raise your hand if you want to be **wealthy**," most people would raise their hand and probably shout "YES!" Let's look at the Bible's definition of **wealthy**.

Wealthy—**Jehovah Chayil**—means power, wealth, and army. It indicates a place of protection, a sanctuary, or security. It also means strength, force, power, valor, and worthiness.

Understand, God is not opposed to His children being wealthy. However, the first **posture** of being wealthy is being grounded in God, unshaken by the possibility of being pulled away. **He alone** is the source of our wealth, as He has given us the gifts and talents that produce abundance.

Look at the steps in the scripture above:

1. You tested us; You refined us like silver;
2. You brought us into the net and laid burdens on our backs;
3. You let people ride over our heads;

4. We went through fire and water;
5. But You have brought us to a wealthy place.
   Trust God's process to your wealthy place.

PROSPER

Jeremiah 29:11

*"For I know the plans I have for you, declares the LORD, plans
to prosper you and not to harm you, plans to give you hope
and a future."*

Daily Acronym

Prayer Renews Our Soul Perfecting Empowering Revelation

Everybody shout boldly—"God's plan is not to harm me!"
Say it again, and again! So many times, when we are in a season of
testing, trial, or temptation, we view it as if God is trying to harm us.
Why would He do that if He said He loves us? People of God, **wake
up**—His ways are **not** like our ways.

What we call a **test**, God refers to as **preparation** for the
blessing. Most of God's preparation for the blessing begins with a
renewing of our minds—the soul part of the triune man. We must
grow and evolve in God's ways to understand the **wiles** of the enemy,
to withstand the voices of deception, and to recognize the voice of God.
The Bible clearly tells us, "In our own eyes we think we are wise," but
not in the things of God. We are **ever learning** about our strengths and
weaknesses.

Reminder—The Bible says, "A just man falls seven times, but
he gets up." Allow the completion of God's work in your life. Every
day, remind yourself, "What God is allowing in my life has His plan
and purpose, and it is **not** meant to harm me."

"Lord, reveal to me what You are perfecting in me."
Prayer Renews Our Soul Perfecting Empowering Revelation.

HEART

Psalm 73:26

"My flesh and my heart may fail, but God is the strength of my heart and my portion forever."

Daily Acronym

His Ear Attentively Receives Truth

In life, we grow up—well, some of us grow up—with the mindset of "I can't wait till I get grown." Let me speak for myself—that was definitely my mindset when my parents were correcting or disciplining me. I'd roll my eyes—just the wrong attitude.

Then, after giving my life to God, I didn't realize that learning God's ways required the responsibility of being **disciplined**. Additionally, adulthood and life itself require discipline in every area. Furthermore, all our thoughts, emotions, and actions come straight from the condition of our **hearts**. I used to think the heart was just something that beat!

The Bible clearly states that "out of the heart flow the issues of life." My question to you today is: **How do you handle life?** Do you go through each day reacting to disappointments, anxiety, frustration, anger, hopelessness, or depression? These feelings are exhausting even to name. All of these are the result of the condition of **your heart**.

Today—Make a decision to commit yourself to allowing God to **discipline** your mindset and realign your heart so that you may reap the rewards He has available for you in His Word.

He hears our every cry, and He said, "In your weakness, I will be your strength."

LATE

2 Peter 3:9 (MSG)

*"God isn't late with His promise, as some measure lateness. He
is restraining Himself on account of you, holding back the end
because He doesn't want anyone lost. He's giving everyone
space and time to change."*

Daily Acronym

Listen Attentively Trusting Emmanuel

If we took a poll of Kingdom believers who have been or are in
a season of **waiting**, **trusting**, **trying**, or **testing**, I guarantee that we
have all experienced the emotional rollercoaster of saying, "Lord,
You're not going to answer me—it's going to be too late." **Let the
church say amen!**

Even though we know God is **omnipotent**, **omniscient**, and
omnipresent, when we face what we call a crisis or emergency, we tend
to doubt God's ability to answer our cries.

Times like these remind us to know the **truth** of God's Word—
that He is with us in the valley, He will **never** leave nor forsake us, and
while we are yet calling, He is sending an answer. The **waiting** is
producing the **fruit** of patience and trust, ripening our lives for future
dimensions in God and life's experiences.

Stop listening to the voices of the enemy or your own
emotions. **Declare** and trust in the promises of God—**He is not slack
concerning His promise as we measure lateness!**

Listen Attentively Trusting Emmanuel.

WORRY

Philippians 4:6 (NLT)

"Don't worry about anything; instead, pray about everything. Tell God what you need and thank Him for all He has done."

Daily Acronym

Willfully Overthrowing Rhetoric Resisting Yeshua

Worry—the biblical definition—is a sense of uneasiness and anxiety about the future. Scripture indicates that such anxiety is ultimately grounded in a lack of trust in God and His purposes.

Let the people say, "Sounds about right." Say with me, Worry is an indicator of my level of faith and trust in God. "Help thou my unbelief."

And yes, this is for all the people reading this who are saying, "This can't be talking about me." Yes, you too.

The Bible makes it known that God has given us **His weapons** to use when we are in battle. The scripture states that the weapons of our warfare are mighty through God for pulling down strongholds. **Willfully overthrow** that stronghold.

Concern is content with human limitations. Be content in knowing that God will always come through for His children and give us the victory.

STRENGTH

Psalm 73:26 (NIV)

"My flesh and my heart may fail, but God is the strength of my heart and my portion forever."

Daily Acronym

Steadfast Trust Renewing Empowering Newness Guides Transforms Honors

As children of God, the Bible makes it clear that our flesh is constantly at war with our spirit. However, the Lord has given us the **power** to overrule the flesh. But we need to understand that we cannot do so without the **grace**, power, and **strength** of Almighty God.

It's not just about physical strength. On our journey through life, we need strength in every area—spiritually, physically, financially, emotionally, mentally, and relationally. Thus, we need the **grace** and **strength** of God in all aspects of our lives.

Strength is defined in the Bible as a place or means of **safety**, **protection**, **refuge**, or **stronghold**. The root word of strength means to be strong, to prevail, to make firm, and to **strengthen**.

The words of the song remind us:

"God is the joy and strength of my life; He moves all pain, misery, and strife."

So, search within your innermost being and remind yourself: "My flesh and my heart may fail, but **God is the strength of my heart and my portion forever!**"

HARLOT

Proverbs 5:3

"For the lips of a harlot are like a honeycomb dripping, and her throat is smoother than oil."

Daily Acronym

Having A Revelatory Love Of Truth

Now, I know you might frown at the word **harlot**. However, in biblical times, being a **harlot** was a common occurrence, although the Bible clearly teaches that this behavior is wrong.

One of my favorite people in the Bible is **Rahab**, a harlot. Why? She was living the life she knew at that time. Girlfriend was making money; she had no view of a better life. However, she **heard** about the mighty acts of deliverance the Lord had done at the Red Sea. This is a reminder that the opportunity to know who **God** is will be revealed to every person, and it's our choice to surrender our lives to Him.

Even though Rahab was a **harlot**, she was also a businesswoman who understood the power of **choice**. She recognized the **God** in the men of God who stood before her. Because of her **choice**, God transformed her life, and Rahab became part of the genealogy of **Jesus**, our Lord and Savior.

A **harlot** is a woman who gives herself to men for money—a prostitute. But here's the beauty: **God still loves you**, and He can transform your life. The **choice** is yours.

HARVEST

"While the earth remains, seedtime and harvest, and cold and heat, and summer and winter, and day and night shall not cease."

Daily Acronym

Having Attained Released Empowering Steadfast Trust

The word **harvest** in the Bible pertains to several areas:

1. There are many people who need to be brought to God.
2. There is a proper time when we will reap a harvest if we do not give up.
3. It refers to God's provision for us and God's blessing for others.

So, we can see that **harvest** includes, but is not limited to, what we receive from God.

Today's passage assures us in the **Book of Beginnings** that "while the earth remains, there will always be **seedtime and harvest.**" Yet, if we are honest, during the **time** or the **waiting** season—when we are told to "wait on the Lord and be of good courage"—our emotions often become overwhelmed with doubt, fear, and unbelief.

I encourage you today, in your season of **waiting**, to sow a seed of encouragement to others, because a seed will never leave your life.

Declare—Harvest is a promise of God as long as the earth remains!

While you wait for the manifestation of your **harvest**, declare God's Word with authority, spend time in worship, share the Word with others, and pray without ceasing, knowing God watches over His Word to perform it.

CONQUER

Deuteronomy 28:7

"The Lord will conquer your enemies when they attack you."

Daily Acronym

Christians Overcome Naysayers Quickly Unfolding Established Redemption

To **conquer** means to defeat an enemy or take control of a foreign land. As believers, we should walk confidently, knowing that **God**—in all His triune power—has the ability to defeat anything that comes our way.

Today, let's conquer doubt and build ourselves up in our most holy faith. The scriptures following verse 7 outline the fullness of God's promises:

Verse 8—The Lord will "guarantee" a blessing on **everything** you do and will **fill** your storehouses with grain. The Lord your God **will** bless you in the land He is giving you.

This alone should cause you to **burst forth in praise** to Almighty God!

Hallelujah! To God be the glory for the things He has already done, prepared, and set forth in His Word for His children.

All God wants from us is a **yes**—**yes** to His will and way; **yes** to hiding His promises in our hearts, which establishes hope, trust, and confidence that we can **conquer** anything with God as our guide.

TRANSFORMED

Romans 12:2

"Stop imitating the ideals and opinions of the culture around you, but be inwardly transformed by the Holy Spirit through a total reformation of how you think. This will empower you to discern God's will as you live a beautiful life, satisfying and perfect in His eyes."

Daily Acronym

Truth Revealed Activates Now Steadfastly Focusing On Renewed Mindset Every Day

The Greek word for **transformed** in Romans 12:2 means being **changed into another form**.

The scripture is clear:

- Stop imitating the ideals and opinions of the culture around you.
- Be **inwardly** transformed by the Holy Spirit.
- Be transformed by a total reformation of how you **think**.
- This will **empower** you to discern God's will.

Today, examine your **beliefs**. Do they align with God's **Word**, or are they just influenced by life experiences and the world around you? The assurance of knowing that **your life** pleases God comes from examining your beliefs and being conscious and intentional about aligning your life with **God's decrees**.

Declutter your mind and **activate** the **truth** of God's Word. It will position your life for the blessings of the Lord that make you rich!

PERSEVERES

James 1:12

"Blessed is the one who perseveres under trial because, having stood the test, that person will receive the crown of life that the Lord has promised to those who love him."

Daily Acronym

Pursuing   Exalted   Reigning   Savior   Enduring Various Extremities Resiliently Expecting Success

To **persevere** in the Bible means to remain persistent despite difficulties or delays. **Read that again!** The Word of God teaches us that "we must believe that He is and that He is a rewarder of those who diligently seek Him."

Whenever we face difficulties, don't think for one moment that **God** is unaware. Remember, **God** told Satan, "Have you considered my servant Job?" God is fully aware of the tests we face. **Trust**—He is developing His strength in us.

Jesus—God's **only Son**—did not escape the difficulties and tests that proved His power and might, giving us the assurance to **trust** in the strength of our God.

"Blessed is the one who perseveres." So, whatever difficulties or tests you might be facing today, **pursue**! Fill your mind and heart with the **living** promises of God. They will strengthen you through the process. Be resiliently expecting success because **God never fails**!

HONOR

1 Samuel 2:30 (NIV)

"Therefore the Lord, the God of Israel, declares: 'I promised that members of your family would minister before me forever.' But now the Lord declares: 'Far be it from me! Those who honor me I will honor, but those who despise me will be disdained.'"

Daily Acronym

Having Our Needs Overseen Repeatedly

To **honor** God means to live a life that reflects respect, reverence, and obedience to Him. When we honor God in our words, thoughts, and actions, He honors us in return by fulfilling His promises and meeting our needs.

God is faithful to **oversee** every detail of our lives when we walk in **honor** toward Him. He will not only provide for you but will elevate you in ways that bring **glory** to His name. Choose to honor God in all you do, and you will experience His **unfailing favor**.

SHIFT

1 Kings 11:2 (NET)

"They came from nations about which the Lord had warned the Israelites, 'You must not establish friendly relations with them! If you do, they will surely shift your allegiance to their gods.' But Solomon was irresistibly attracted to them."

Daily Acronym

Stand Humble In Faith Trusting

A **shift** can be a dangerous moment in our spiritual journey when we allow influences to pull us away from God's direction. God warns us to stay vigilant in our relationships and choices because they can **shift** our focus away from Him.

Examine your life and be mindful of anything that might be causing a **shift** in your allegiance to God. Stay rooted in His Word, **trust** Him completely, and stand firm in your faith, allowing no distractions to pull you off course.

PROCESS

Jeremiah 18:4 (NIV)

"But the pot he was shaping from the clay was marred in his hands; so the potter formed it into another pot, shaping it as seemed best to him."

Daily Acronym

Principles Repeated Ongoing Creates Establishes Secures Success

God is constantly shaping us, much like a potter shapes clay. We are all in a continual **process** of growth, refinement, and transformation. While we may feel marred or broken at times, God sees the finished product, and He is committed to shaping us into His image.

Be patient with the **process**. God is not finished with you yet! Each step, whether joyful or challenging, is part of His plan to create something beautiful and useful in your life. Trust His timing, and know that this **ongoing process** will secure your success in Him.

BLOOM

Isaiah 61:11 (MSG)

"For as the earth bursts with spring wildflowers, and as a garden cascades with blossoms, so the Master, God brings righteousness into full bloom and puts praise on display before the nations."

Daily Acronym

Becoming Like Our Obedient Messiah

Just like flowers bloom in their season, God desires for us to **bloom** in righteousness. Our growth and transformation are a reflection of His work in our lives, and when we live in obedience, we become a display of His glory for the world to see.

Are you in a season of blooming? Stay connected to God, and allow His Spirit to continue the work He has started in you. As you **bloom**, your life will reflect His goodness and bring praise to His name, showing others the beauty of living in Christ.

JUMP

Psalm 18:29 (NET)

"Indeed, with your help I can charge against an army; by my God's power, I can jump over a wall."

Daily Acronym

Jesus Undergirds My Prayers

With God's power, nothing is impossible! He gives us the strength and courage to overcome any obstacle or barrier in our path. When challenges seem too great, remember that God's power enables you to **jump** over them.

Whatever walls you are facing, know that God is on your side. Trust in His strength, and take that **leap of faith**. God will help you **jump** over every obstacle that stands in the way of your victory.

ORDAINED

Psalm 139:16 (NIV)

"Your eyes saw my unformed body; all the days ordained for me were written in your book before one of them came to be."

Daily Acronym

Ordered, Restored, Directed And Instructed Now Exalted Divine

God has **ordained** every day of your life. Before you were born, He had a plan for you, a purpose for each moment. Even when life feels chaotic or uncertain, you can rest in the knowledge that God's divine plan is **ordered** and **directed** for your good.

Trust in God's **ordination** over your life. He is leading you, restoring what was lost, and directing you into His perfect will. As you follow His instructions, you will see His plan come to fruition, and you will be **exalted** in His timing.

FLOURISH

Psalm 92:12 (TPT)

"Yes! Look how you've made all your devoted lovers to flourish like palm trees, each one growing in victory, standing with strength!"

Daily Acronym

Faithful Living Overcomes Underestimating Righteousness Inspiring Strength and Hope

To **flourish** means to grow abundantly, to thrive in all areas of life. God promises that those who are devoted to Him will flourish like trees planted by streams of water. This **growth** is not just in physical prosperity but also in spiritual strength, hope, and righteousness.

As you remain **faithful** to God, you will see your life **flourish** in ways you never imagined. Trust in His promises, and know that your devotion to Him will lead to victory and strength. Allow your life to inspire others as a testament to God's faithfulness.

TRANSFORM

Romans 12:2 (NIV)

"Do not conform to the pattern of this world, but be transformed by the renewing of your mind. Then you will be able to test and approve what God's will is—His good, pleasing and perfect will."

Daily Acronym

Truth Reveals All Necessary Steps For Ongoing Renewed Mindset

Transformation begins from within. As we allow God's **truth** to penetrate our hearts and minds, we experience a complete shift in the way we think and live. This **transformation** is not just a one-time event but an ongoing process as we renew our minds with the Word of God.

Let His **truth** guide you daily as you seek to live a life that reflects His will. Be intentional about what you focus on and let God's Word shape your thoughts, actions, and attitudes, creating a lasting transformation.

ENEMY

Matthew 5:44 (TPT)

"But I say, love your enemy! Bless the one who curses you, do something wonderful for the one who hates you, and respond to the very ones who persecute you by praying for them."

Daily Acronym

Effectively Nullifying Enmity Motivates You

Jesus commands us to **love** our enemies, a challenging but crucial aspect of our faith. When we choose to respond to hate with love, we **nullify** enmity, break the cycle of anger, and reflect Christ's character.

Loving your **enemy** can transform not only your heart but also your relationships. It's not an easy task, but it brings healing and growth. Take a step today to pray for those who oppose you, and allow God to work through your acts of love and kindness.

WALK

Micah 6:8 (NIV)

"He has shown you, O mortal, what is good. And what does the Lord require of you? To act justly and to love mercy and to walk humbly with your God."

Daily Acronym

Wisdom Activates Living Kingdom-style

Your **walk** with God is a reflection of how you live your life. God requires us to walk in humility, love, and justice, aligning our actions with His kingdom principles. This journey with God is not just about belief, but about how we live out that belief every day.

Let your **walk** be a testament to your faith. Seek God's wisdom in every decision and step, allowing His love and justice to guide you. In doing so, your life will reflect His kingdom on earth, and you will be a light to others.

OVERWHELMED

Psalm 61:2 (NIV)

"From the ends of the earth I call to you, I call as my heart grows faint; lead me to the rock that is higher than I."

Daily Acronym

Ordained Vigilance Enables Resilience, Warring Hope Evokes Loving Master's Expected Deliverance

Life can feel overwhelming at times, but even in those moments, God is our refuge. When you are **overwhelmed**, call on Him. He is the Rock, higher than your fears, and stronger than any storm you face.

When your heart is heavy and your strength is failing, trust that God is with you. He will give you the **resilience** you need to endure and the hope to keep moving forward. Lean into His presence, and allow Him to lead you to peace and deliverance.

WHY

"That is why, for Christ's sake, I delight in weaknesses, in insults, in hardships, in persecutions, in difficulties. For when I am weak, then I am strong."

Daily Acronym

Willfully Humbly Yield

We often ask **why** when we face hardship, but the answer lies in God's plan for our growth and His strength being perfected in our weakness. When we **yield** to God in moments of trial, we experience His power working through us in ways we could never imagine.

Instead of asking **why**, ask God what He wants to teach you in your trials. His strength is made perfect in your weakness, and His grace is sufficient. Yield to His will, knowing that He is with you, and His purpose is for your good.

BUT

Matthew 24:13 (NIV)

"But the one who stands firm to the end will be saved."

Daily Acronym

Bold Undeniable Truth

The word **but** introduces contrast, a turning point in a statement or situation. In the face of adversity, Jesus reminds us to stand firm. No matter what comes, **truth** remains, and the end result is **salvation** for those who persevere.

When you face opposition or doubt, remember the power of God's **truth**. Stand on His promises, and let no **but** of fear or discouragement sway you from your path. His **truth** will always prevail.

SWORD

Ephesians 6:17 (NIV)

"Take the helmet of salvation and the sword of the Spirit, which is the word of God."

Daily Acronym

Spoken Words Orchestrate Relentless Defeat

God's Word is a powerful weapon against the enemy. The **sword** of the Spirit, which is the Word of God, allows us to cut through lies, doubt, and fear, declaring **victory** in the spiritual battles we face.

Use the **sword** of the Word daily, speaking it over your life and circumstances. It is your defense and your offense, and it never fails. When you feel under attack, turn to the **Word** and let it fight on your behalf.

PREPARED

Psalm 31:19 (AMP)

"How great is Your goodness, which You have stored up for those who fear You, which You have prepared for those who take refuge in You, before the sons of men!"

Daily Acronym

Pray, Read, Exalt, Praise, And Repeat Every Day Diligently

God has **prepared** great blessings and goodness for those who seek refuge in Him. His provisions are already stored up, waiting for us to walk in faith and trust.

To access what God has **prepared** for you, live in a posture of prayer, reading His Word, and praising Him continually. By doing so, you are aligning yourself with His will and readying yourself for the blessings He has stored up.

GRACE

2 Corinthians 12:9 (NIV)

"But he said to me, 'My grace is sufficient for you, for my power is made perfect in weakness.' Therefore I will boast all the more gladly about my weaknesses, so that Christ's power may rest on me."

Daily Acronym

God's Refreshing Anointing Covers Everything

God's **grace** is not just a gift, but a sustaining force that empowers us in our weakness. When we come to the end of ourselves, His strength takes over. It's in our weakest moments that His power is most clearly revealed.

Embrace your need for God's **grace**. It covers every mistake, every shortcoming, and every challenge. In those moments when you feel powerless, remind yourself that His **grace** is more than enough to carry you through.

RESTORE

Jeremiah 30:17 (NIV)

*"But I will restore you to health and heal your wounds,'
declares the Lord, 'because you are called an outcast, Zion for
whom no one cares.'"*

Daily Acronym

Rebuking Every Satanic Trial Opens Renewal and Elevation

God is in the business of **restoration**. Whether physical, emotional, or spiritual wounds, He promises to heal and restore His people. Even when we feel forgotten or abandoned, He cares deeply for us and works to make us whole again.

Trust in God's promise to **restore** every area of your life that has been broken or hurt. He is faithful, and His healing power knows no bounds. Hold on to His Word, and watch as He brings renewal and elevation into your life.

TREE

Matthew 7:17 (NIV)

"Likewise, every good tree bears good fruit, but a bad tree bears bad fruit."

Daily Acronym

Totally Renew Every Experience

We are likened to **trees** in scripture, and just as a tree is known by its fruit, so are we known by our actions and character. Good fruit comes from a life rooted in God, while bad fruit reveals areas of life that need correction and renewal.

Examine the **fruit** in your life. Are your actions and words reflecting the goodness of God? If not, allow God to prune and **renew** you so that every experience and interaction is filled with His presence and bears fruit that brings Him glory.

WAR

Psalm 144:1 (NIV)

"Praise be to the Lord my Rock, who trains my hands for war, my fingers for battle."

Daily Acronym

Wise Anointed Resilience

God prepares us for the battles we face in life. Though we may not fight with physical weapons, we engage in spiritual warfare daily, and He equips us with wisdom and strength. Our **resilience** comes from His training and His empowerment.

Every day, put on the full armor of God and trust in His training. He has already equipped you to face whatever comes your way, and with His anointing, you are prepared for victory in every battle.

WARRIORS

"Proclaim this among the nations: Prepare for war! Rouse the warriors! Let all the fighting men draw near and attack." Joel 3:9 (NIV)

Daily Acronym

Withstanding Adversity, Relentless Resilience Increases Strength

We are called to be **warriors** in the kingdom of God. This means standing firm in our faith, fighting the battles we face with relentless **resilience**, and relying on God's strength. Spiritual warfare is real, but we are not defenseless; God has equipped us with everything we need.

Every morning, prepare for the spiritual battles ahead. Arm yourself with prayer, the Word, and unwavering faith, and step into your day with the confidence that you are a **warrior** in God's army, ready to stand against any attack.

About The Author

Dr. Renee' A. Meeks

Co-Pastor Dr. Renee' Antoinette Meeks is a native of West Palm Beach, Florida. She is the only daughter born to Raymond Atkins and Fannie Whisenant Jones. Both parents have departed this life. Co-Pastor Meeks graduated from Twin Lakes High School in West Palm Beach, Florida. She continued her education at Boston University in Boston, MA, and received a Bachelor of Science Degree in Business

Education and a Doctor of Divinity from Elbon-Solutions College of Ministry. Dr. Meeks has been a Mortgage Loan Originator and Underwriter and has assisted families in obtaining funding for homeownership for over 20 years.

Dr. Meeks parents encouraged and required her to attend Payne Chapel AME Church, the seed of the Lord Jesus Christ was sown into her heart at an early age. As a result, in 1982 she accepted the Lord Jesus Christ as her personal savior and was filled with the Holy Ghost in 1985.

As she was standing FIRM in living a sold out single life, God honored her sacrifice and in 1987 she met Apostle Will A. Meeks, and married him on September 3, 1988. This God ordained union STANDS united and committed to each other and to the Lord Jesus Christ as servants of God bringing "restoration to contrite spirits."

Today, Co-Pastor Dr. Meeks serves alongside her husband in ministry as Co- Pastor of Sweet Honey in the Rock Restoration Church which serves the Atlanta metropolitan community. Co-Pastor Meeks, serves as Director of the Women of Resilience, the Women's Alliance, Praise Team Leader, Instructor with School of the Word (Bible Study), and Leads Weekly Corporate Prayer. She also serves on the Evangelistic and Trustee Boards. She is an author and Certified Life Coach.

She is truly **T**ransformed, **H**umbled, **U**ndeniably **G**odly and has a heart to please God and believes "MY PRAYER COUNTS!!"

Notes

Notes

Notes

Notes

Notes

Notes

Notes

Notes

Notes

Notes

Notes